W9-CFJ-398

Let's Learn About LITERATURE

FABLES, MYTHS, AND LEGENDS

Therese M. Shea

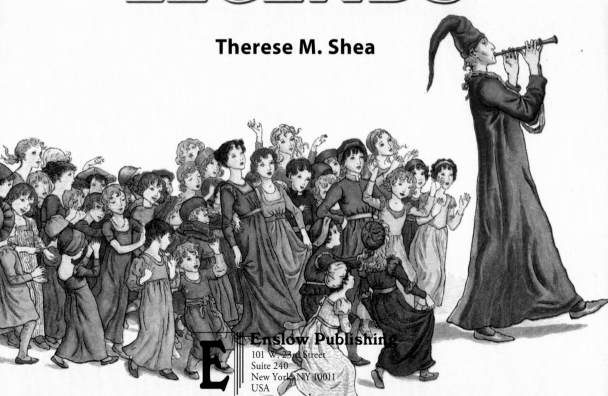

Enslow Publishing
101 W. 23rd Street
Suite 240
New York, NY 10011
USA
enslow.com

WORDS TO KNOW

ancient From a very long time ago.

chariot A cart with two wheels that was pulled by horses in ancient times.

explain To tell or show the reason for something.

feature An important part; to have an important part.

hare A fast animal that looks like a rabbit.

Norsemen The people of ancient Norway, Sweden, Denmark, or Iceland.

punish To make someone suffer for bad actions.

steady Continuing over a long time.

tortoise A kind of turtle that lives on land.

values Important ideas about how we should live and act.

CONTENTS

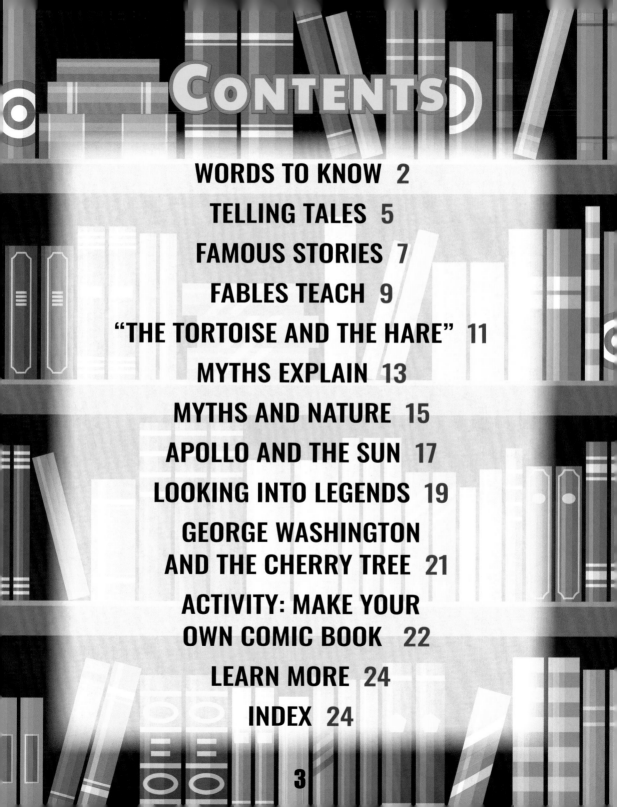

Grandparents pass on stories to their children and grandchildren.

Telling Tales

Some stories tell us about the beliefs or **values** of people. Fables, myths, and legends are stories like these. They have been passed down over many, many years.

FAST FACT

Fables, myths, and legends are ways to look into the past!

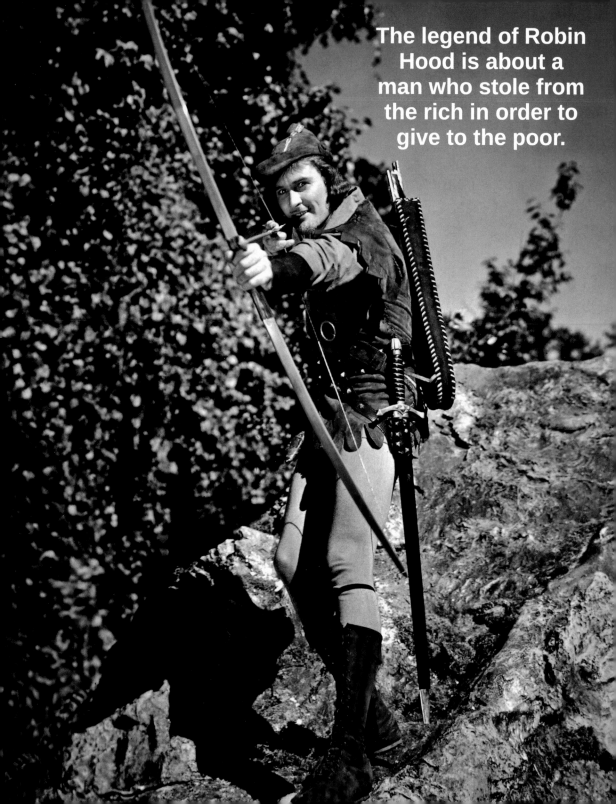

The legend of Robin Hood is about a man who stole from the rich in order to give to the poor.

Famous Stories

Fables, myths, and legends have special **features** that make them different from each other. Many have become famous. You might know some already!

FAST FACT

The story of Robin Hood is a famous legend that has been told in many stories and movies.

Aesop wrote many fables including "The Town Mouse and the Country Mouse" and "The Boy Who Cried Wolf."

Fables Teach

A fable is a story that teaches a lesson. Fables often feature animals that act like people. A Greek slave named Aesop is said to have written many fables.

**"The Tortoise and the Hare"
teaches us to keep going, even
if we are not the best or fastest.**

"The Tortoise and the Hare"

"The **Tortoise** and the **Hare**" is one of Aesop's fables. In it, a hare and tortoise have a race. The hare thinks he will win, so he takes a nap—and loses!

FAST FACT

The lesson in "The Tortoise and the Hare" is "slow but **steady** wins the race."

Thor is a god in Norse myths who carries a powerful hammer.

Myths Explain

Myths are stories about gods and heroes. They often **explain** why things happen. **Ancient** people believed myths were true. There are many myths about how the world was created.

Fast Fact

Ancient Greeks, Romans, Egyptians, Native Americans, and **Norsemen** had myths.

Greek myths say that the god Poseidon created horses.

Myths and Nature

Ancient people did not know about science like we do. They used myths to explain events in nature. Other myths explain where people come from and what happens after death.

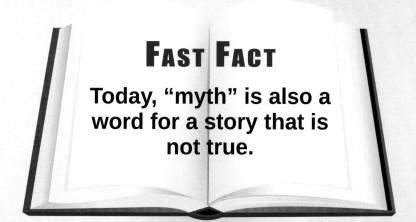

FAST FACT

Today, "myth" is also a word for a story that is not true.

Apollo was known as the god of light and sun.

Apollo and the Sun

Apollo was the son of Zeus, the king of the Greek gods. Each day, Apollo rode a golden **chariot** through the air. This myth explained why the sun moved across the sky.

FAST FACT

Ancient Romans gave many of the Greek gods new names. Zeus was Jupiter to the Romans.

The Pied Piper leads all of the children out of town by playing his magic pipe.

Looking into Legends

Legends are stories about certain places or people. They are told like they are history. A legend often has both true and made-up parts.

FAST FACT

The legend of the Pied Piper tells how he punished a town for not paying him for chasing away rats. He stole their children!

The legend about George Washington and the cherry tree started shortly after he died.

George Washington and the Cherry Tree

One famous legend is about young George Washington. He chopped down a cherry tree. Later, George told his angry father about it. George said he could not tell a lie. But the legend is not true!

FAST FACT

The legend of Washington chopping down the tree tells us that Americans value telling the truth.

Activity

Make Your Own Comic Book

MATERIALS
- paper
- ruler
- pencils

Comic books often feature people doing amazing things, just like in many

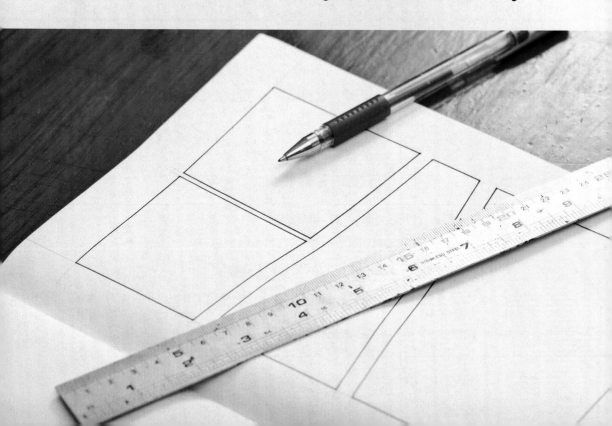

fables, myths, and legends. You can make your own comic book about a fable, myth, or legend!

1. Pick a fable, myth, or legend that you think would make a good comic book. You can find them using the websites at the end of this book or in a book at the library.

2. Draw boxes on white sheets of paper. These will be the spaces in which you will draw and tell the story.

3. Decide what will go in each box— and start making your comic book!

LEARN MORE

Books

Aesop. *The Aesop for Children*. Minneapolis, MN: First Avenue Editions, 2014.

Hoena, Blake. *Epic Adventures of Odysseus: An Interactive Mythological Adventure*. North Mankato, MN: Capstone Press, 2017.

Lock, Deborah. *Myths and Legends*. New York, NY: DK Publishing, 2015.

Websites

Ancient Myths & Folktales for Kids
www.mrdonn.org / stories.html
Read about ancient tales from around the world.

Myths and Legends
www.history-for-kids.com / myths-and-legends.html
Check out myths and poems about famous characters in myths.

INDEX

Published in 2019 by Enslow Publishing, LLC.
101 W. 23rd Street, Suite 240, New York, NY 10011

Copyright © 2019 by Enslow Publishing, LLC.

All rights reserved.

No part of this book may be reproduced by any means without the written permission of the publisher.

Library of Congress Cataloging-in-Publication Data

Names: Shea, Therese, author.
Title: Fables, myths, and legends / Therese M. Shea.
Description: New York, NY : Enslow Publishing, LLC, 2019. | Series: Let's learn about literature | Audience: K to Grade 4. | Includes bibliographical references and index. | Identifiers: LCCN 2017045117 | ISBN 9780766096103 (library bound) | ISBN 9780766095953 (pbk.) | ISBN 9780766095977 (6 pack)
Subjects: LCSH: Fables—Juvenile literature. | Mythology—Juvenile literature. | Legends—Juvenile literature.
Classification: LCC PN980 .S54 2019 | DDC 398.2—dc23
LC record available at https://lccn.loc.gov/2017045117

Printed in the United States of America

To Our Readers: We have done our best to make sure all website addresses in this book were active and appropriate when we went to press. However, the author and the publisher have no control over and assume no liability for the material available on those websites or on any websites they may link to. Any comments or suggestions can be sent by e-mail to customerservice@enslow.com.

Photo Credits: Cover, p. 1 duncan1890/DigitalVision Vectors/Getty Images; pp. 2–3, 24 Gurza/Shutterstock.com; p. 4 Photo Researchers/Science Source/Getty Images; pp. 5, 7, 9, 11, 13, 15, 17, 19, 21, 22–23 (paper, notebook, pencil) narmacero/Shutterstock.com; pp. 5, 7, 11, 15, 17, 19, 21, 22 (open book) Wen Wen/Shutterstock.com; p. 6 Silver Screen Collection/Moviepix/Getty Images; p. 8 Photo 12/Universal Images Group/Getty Images; p. 10 Anton Brand/Shutterstock.com; p. 12 Fotokostic/Shutterstock.com; p. 14 DEA/G. Dagli Orti/De Agostini/Getty Images; p. 16 Lebrecht Music and Arts Photo Library/Alamy Stock Photo; p. 18 Universal Images Group/Getty Images; p. 20 Archive Photos/Getty Images; p. 22 Chaiwuth Wichitdho/Shutterstock.com.